Innocence to Wholeness

Journey of the Heroine

Written and Illustrated by

SHARON RUSSELL

PINK MOMENT PRESS

Published in the United States by
Pink Moment Press
Submit all inquiries at www.sharonrussellart.com

Library of Congress: 2013910697
ISBN: 978-0-9825000-8-8

Illustrations by Sharon Russell
Book design by Suzy Bennitt and Sharon Russell

10 9 8 7 6 5 4 3 2 2015 2014 2013

*made with love
in Ojai, California*

Foreword

It is rare to find the delicate sensitivity of a fine artist who can combine her art with the wisdom of a profound teaching. Sharon Russell's "Dragon Story" does just that. It is a beautiful portrayal of the "Heroine's Journey," a touching story of how each of us comes to make peace with the darker, scary, "shadow" side of ourselves - what Sharon Russell calls the Dragon.

It is easy to see our lives from the point of view of the Heroine's struggle. But what really is her struggle? How do we deal with these unwanted and unloved parts of ourselves, this unwanted Dragon? This is what the psychologist, Carl Jung, called "the Shadow" - the repressed and often hidden parts of ourselves that we are not yet ready to see and accept. These unpleasant parts of our nature are pain, fear, and rejection. Unknowingly, we project these parts onto others, instead of recognizing them as parts of ourselves. Sharon shows us a way that we can use this Shadow-Dragon energy to become our best Self and to truly become the Heroine/Hero of our own life.

Having known Sharon for over twenty years, I have watched her move through her own Dragon process and have been graced by her wise words as I move through mine. I have watched the paintings evolve, and witnessed her struggle with the intensity of the process of creation - from the "aha's" and delights when the ideas, pen and paints were flowing, to the headaches and eye-strain when they weren't. The intensity of her concentration on each painting would almost put her into an altered state of consciousness as she stepped into the picture to bring forth what needed to be expressed. Her attention to color and line is precise, original and meaningful in every detail.

Sharon and I, as therapists and astrologers, recognize the importance of owning one's Shadow-Dragon. It is the story of how we heal - how we must each encounter, understand, and embrace our own inner Dragon. No one is without one. But in this beautifully rendered story, we are shown a gentle way to move through the process to becoming all that we can be - our best Selves.

Whether we are young or old, these images touch us, because somewhere inside each of us we find ourselves in the story. The journey is never done, and Sharon has created a beautiful guide for us.

The psychologist, Carl Jung, once said "It is even better to be whole than to be good." In this book, Sharon teaches us how to be whole by learning to accept and to be at peace with our inner Dragon, and to become that which we already are: the Heroine of our own story.

Elizabeth Spring, M.A.
Author, *North Node Astrology:*
Rediscovering Your Life Direction and Soul Purpose

Introduction

The art that you see created in this book was inspired after a period of illness and depression which was triggered during a visit with relatives where the atmosphere in the house was negative. Upon browsing through bookstores to get some relief, I found a Sleeping Beauty coloring book that transported me back to my childhood and the drawings I used to make at that time. So I bought the book and some crayons, headed back to the guest room and began coloring my heart out. The next day I began to have ideas of my own and started drawing thumbnail sketches. Aware that those Disney Sleeping Beauty, Cinderella, Snow White stories were based on women finding their fulfillment from a man, I began to notice that my sketches were of women inspired on their own. Some images seemed very strong, some seemed very accomplished, some peaceful.

Upon returning home I kept pondering the style and medium I wanted to use. My good friend, Elizabeth Spring, and I were discussing this as we walked down State Street in Santa Barbara, California when low and behold a great moment of synchronicity occurred. There in a store window was a book of angels painted in an ethereal water color style. I had not done water color before but knew that would be my medium to create the loose feeling I wanted which I thought would contrast well with a very accurate and detailed drawing. I later discovered that adding colored pencil enhanced the details best.

Using my past experience as a graphic designer, artist, and psychotherapist, I painted many archetypal images of women before I realized I wanted to create a story of the Heroine's or Hero's Journey. The Ten Ox- herding pictures from the 12th century with their story done in the tradition of Zen Buddhism illustrating the stages of progression toward enlightenment by searching for, finding, taming, riding and eventually forgetting about the ox was very inspiring to me. Also, from the western world we have Carl Jung's idea of the shadow which is the memories, repressions and even untapped talents and gifts that reside in the unconscious. The process of becoming aware of what lies in our unconscious can be used in the journey toward wholeness. The symbol that came to me for this journey was the Dragon. Like the ox, the Dragon would need some taming.

It is important to realize that the journey from Innocence to Wholeness is not a straight path, and is a lifelong journey. I often find myself revisiting certain images over and over again. In fact, Sanctuary is very important and those of us who can create a little quiet time or meditation every day will benefit greatly. Put your Dragon or worries in a box and don't allow yourself to be overwhelmed by the shadow or Dragon. Slowly learn to connect with this aspect of your psyche.

After having sold many Dragon story illustrations in card form, I began to wonder if I should put it into a book, but I never moved in that direction because it always seemed too difficult. Then another wonderful thing happened. An amazing woman, Suzy Bennitt, called me one day asking if she could come up to Ojai to see my work. Her enthusiasm, appreciation of art and transpersonal psychology affected me very positively. As our friendship grew, we began to talk about creating the book. Suzy's creative abilities are many and included a past experience with helping another person put their story into a book. This book would not have come about without her.

With love and light,

Sharon Russell

Sharon Russell, M.A.
Author and Artist

an Invitation

As you view and read this book, you may find it helpful to meditate on a certain image that you especially resonate with or that you want to experience more fully.

A simple meditation you can do is breathe through and focus on your heart area. Place a hand over your heart and breathe slowly until you feel balanced and calm. Now take yourself back in time to a memory when you felt happy, loved, appreciated or cared for, and re-experience that memory. As much as possible, remember smells, color or sound - whatever you can recall that is positive.

Now look at the illustration again - be with it and ask yourself a question, such as "Help me to learn more about courage and setting boundaries." This could be in regards to a special situation or a certain person you are having trouble with. Or you might mediate on Sanctuary, for instance, "Help me to find time to create an inner, maybe even outer, Sanctuary." After the question, be still and listen. Answers may come now or anytime later. Patience is key.

Remember, this journey isn't always linear. You may find yourself going back to certain images over and over again or skipping around. Also, for some people, journaling your thoughts after being with an image is another way to access a deeper connection with yourself.

Innocence

*I*NNNOCENCE is the state we are in before we have been wounded or victimized by life. We have the qualities of OPENNESS, TRUST, a RECEPTIVITY to the world.

*H*ere our young Heroine does not see the Dragon behind her. She has no idea of the Dragon's existence or what is about to transpire.

Beauty and the Beast

At some point in our lives we are taken advantage of, abused, hurt, scared, cheated and lied to. It may be in the form of one or several traumatic experiences, or many small injustices, one piled upon another. Here our Heroine feels frightened, small, incapable, helpless and powerless. She feels VICTIMIZED in the face of these harsh forces of her life.

We don't focus on an image that seems fearful or try to make it more intense, rather we acknowledge that we have fears and that they need to come up naturally. We also don't try to force our fears to go away. The safety net of a trusted group or therapist where we can share our experience provides a container for these archetypal energies.

In Search of the Dragon

What will we do after we have been wounded? We may stay small, afraid and helpless; remain in the place of the victim. We may try to distract ourselves from our wounds through an addiction like drugs, alcohol, overeating, TV, etc. Or we may identify with the perpetrator or Dragon and become a bully ourself by victimizing others. Here our Heroine has chosen to prepare herself for meeting the Dragon. She has a sword for protection and a light to see in the darkness.

This picture is symbolic of the help we need in order to uncover and face our hidden wounds which we find in our unconscious or underworld, where we store our memories and past experiences. The LIGHT and SWORD represent GUIDANCE, HELP and SUPPORT of trusted friends or family, a therapist, church or support group.

Community

*T*his journey is a personal exploration, yet finding a COMMUNITY where you feel safe knowing that others also have to deal with the inner and outer struggles of life, knowing you are not alone, is an essential part of the process.

*S*haring your story in a confidential setting, praying together, meditation, chanting, singing, positive rituals can all be a part of the healing.

Courage

It takes COURAGE and strength to face fears, old wounded memories, and our perpetrators. Our Heroine may be afraid, but she pushes on. She stands up straight, willing to commit to do what it takes to not remain in the place of the victim. She is learning to take responsibility for herself, make her own decisions, say what she wants and needs, take action and be a WARRIOR. Drawing lines, SETTING BOUNDARIES, saying no, standing up for her rights, being assertive, she is learning to protect and take care of herself.

Reflection

She looks in the mirror, expecting to see her own REFLECTION. Instead, she sees the Dragon. Surprised and shocked, our Heroine wonders what this could mean. Is the Dragon a part of her? Surrounding her and the Dragon are thorns and roses. A bitter-sweet experience of seeing how beauty and ugliness, softness and sharpness are connected; how opposites can come from the same place, like the two sides of a coin.

Can we own our inner Dragon or do we find ourselves PROJECTING our strength or bully onto others? We cannot love or hate something about another person unless it reflects something we love or hate about ourself -- others are merely MIRRORS of ourself.

Sanctuary

*E*xhausted from the journey, tired and in need of inner peace, our Heroine RETREATS TO A SAFE PLACE. She finds or creates her inner SANCTUARY through visualization, meditation and prayer. It is important at these times to put your Dragon in a box, and let him or her sleep while you become spiritually refreshed.

*H*ere she is safe to SURRENDER TO THE PROCESS, not to another person's demands. This is like finding the key that opens the locked door. She does not know what the outcome will be, but is willing to let go of her personal desires and fears long enough to be in a process that will lead her to a saner, more balanced life.

Understanding

Our Heroine is ready to continue on her journey, arming herself this time with new information. What is there to learn and UNDERSTAND about Dragons? Dragons seem primitive, instinctual, have fire, energy, are independent, strong, and ready to take action. These traits can be used positively to create or protect, or they can be used negatively to bully or destroy. She learns the importance of being honest with herself, acknowledging her shortcomings without guilt, grandiosity, or blaming others.

Accepting our humanness, dragon-ness is one of the most healing things that we can do; to accept that we cannot be perfect, but that we can change or MAKE AMENDS when we have done something that hurts another. There is a Zen idea that goes something like this: "I change not by trying to be what I am not, but by being fully aware of how I am."

Compassion

As a result of opening her mind to new information, her heart is then opened. The Dragon and Heroine make amends and become friends, having COMPASSION for one another. Instead of fearing their differences, their oppositeness, they are learning about the pluses of her receptive energies and his active energies. Learning to forgive ourself and others becomes an important step. Forgiveness does not mean that I approve of the hurtful things that you did to me, or that I will allow you to do them to me again, but rather that I want to LET GO OF OBSESSIVE THOUGHTS about what you or what I have done; I want to let go of my pain. I want to release the poison that can be created from long held guilt or resentment.

Transformation

*U*nderstanding and Compassion, this change in attitude leads to a TRANSFORMATION, a rebirth in the way the Dragon and Heroine relate to one another. Our Heroine is learning more about the pluses of the Dragon's ability to take ACTION, be passionate, stand up after being knocked down. Likewise, the Dragon is learning more about the pluses of taking a break, being RECEPTIVE and quiet, being considerate.

*T*his new way of working together is symbolized by the butterfly wings. The Heroine is now able to HARNESS the Dragon's aggressive energy into an assertive and loving form. This is the beginning of a lifelong job, learning from our mistakes and choosing to do better, knowing we will never become perfect.

Treasures

Having made a positive connection with her inner strength, the Dragon's energy is now a source of guidance and support, showing our Heroine all kinds of TREASURES, gifts, and undeveloped talents that have been hidden in her unconscious. She realizes now that she has always had the tools and resources she has needed, and, that with time she will learn how to use them.

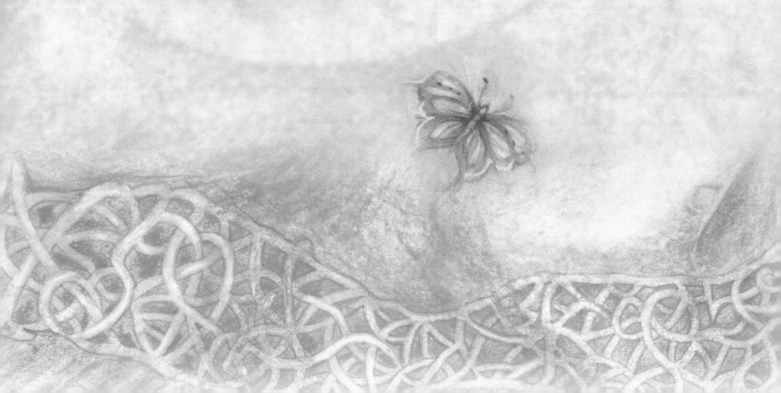

Soaring

The Dragon and Heroine are flying together, working together, enjoying life. When we are not at war with INNER STRUGGLES, expending energy hiding our fears and our wounds from ourself or others, then we discover that we have more energy. When we are able to walk away or create a new attitude about our OUTER STRUGGLES, we will also have more energy and can learn to SOAR!

Wholeness

*I*n WHOLENESS, the opposites can be understood, used together, respected, integrated, or simply watched without judgment. Here our Heroine becomes the WITNESS, is being both receptive and active, is able to hold the container for hurt and acceptance, anger and courage. She evokes the energies of the Higher or Wise Self within her which brings forth knowledge of when to act, when to let go. Here the Blue Dragon symbolizes her softer, more accepting part, while the Red Dragon symbolizes her active, courageous part. She holds these polarities as she uses the Serenity Prayer from Alcoholics Anonymous: "Grant me Serenity to ACCEPT the things I cannot change, COURAGE to change the things I can, and WISDOM to know the difference."

Remember...

Be Gentle With Yourself

Acknowledgements

I would like to thank my husband, Joe, for his many years of patience with me and my art projects which were usually all over the house. His appreciation and support have helped me immensely. And thanks to my dear friend, Elizabeth Spring, whose encouragement helped me to re-enter the art world. Deepest gratitude to my sister, Dixie Gladstone, for all her support and for putting my art on her very creative website, FeminineAstrology.com. Special thanks goes to my longest time friend, Terry Royce, for her ideas and for promoting my work to her many friends. And last but not least, a most special acknowledgment to Suzy Bennitt, the person responsible for so much love and hard work to actually create this book, and her husband, Bob, his company, Pace Marketing Communications, and Pink Moment Press.

For my beloved husband, Joe Zorskie.
You are my rock, fire, water and air.

A Note from the Publisher

I first connected with Sharon Russell and her exquisite art on a fresh Spring day in 2011. I had been in the garden writing a story about a magical woman who lives in the Amazon jungle with her white panther friend. When I walked into the house, I glanced over at an art card, **"TrailBlazer,"** that I had purchased months earlier. Suddenly I realized with great excitement that the beautiful image depicted the very essence of the woman I had been writing about! The artist's painting had met my story in a "dream field" and sprouted into another expression of itself.

On the back of the card, I read that it was *"made with love in Ojai."* Without hesitation, I called the artist to let her know how much her magnificent painting had affected me. I was soon to discover that there were many others who had been profoundly touched by Sharon's creations.

Sharon explained that the source of her art comes from the place of dreams and visions, fairy tales and myths. I believe that people feel an instant connection with Sharon's images because they emerge from the unconscious collective that can be experienced within each of us. They speak to the truth of who we are and how we can develop into a sense of greater wholeness. This invaluable "guidebook" can help us make peace with our shadow self and live more fully in our radiant power.

My wish is that this book be an inspiration and comfort to you. You are not alone on this journey. We all have dragons to reckon with, both inner and outer. However, by keeping good company with loved ones and taking spiritual sustenance from inspirational work like this, we can befriend our dragons and make the most of this precious life!

Wishing you a beautiful journey!

Suzy Bennitt

Suzy Bennitt, M.A.
Publisher, Pink Moment Press

"TrailBlazer"

Reflections

About Sharon Russell

Sharon Russell grew up in the Pacific Northwest with three siblings, her lumberjack father, and mother from New York City. She loved the green trees and grass of the forests and the beautiful colorful flowers her sophisticated mother planted around their house; and these images often show up in her work. Sharon has also always been intrigued with the beauty and mystery of the archetypal images of the feminine.

As a child she felt an intense connection with the Virgin Mary and loved to say prayers next to statues and pictures of her in church. After graduating from Cal State Long Beach, Sharon worked for about 10 years in the graphic design field in Los Angeles, California while painting and creating serigraphs. No longer satisfied to just do beautiful images, she began to ask herself "what is my message?"--with no immediate answer.

Eventually, Sharon went back to school to study Jungian and Transpersonal Psychology and was a psychotherapist for 15 years, during which time she participated in women's groups, some of which had themes of the goddess. Then one day in 1999, she began to be flooded with images of the feminine that had an uplifting and inspiring message. Many watercolor paintings later, the idea of using the Dragon to explain the story of the shadow and individuation were created.

Sharon has lived in Ojai, California since 1983 and continues to create her storybook-mythological watercolor images. Her images can be bought in card form or prints. You can see Sharon and her art on YouTube by searching: "Sharon Russell Ojai Artist." Her art is featured on FeminineAstrology.com, a website created by Sharon's sister, Dixie Gladstone.

SharonRussellArt.com
sharonrussell64@gmail.com

Made in the USA
San Bernardino, CA
06 February 2014

A Journey of Personal Growth

"In this book, our inner and outer dragons are portrayed in a series of colorful, archetypal images that capture your soul. It will show you a way of gentleness and kindness with yourself as you take your journey toward wholeness, a lifelong process. You will discover aspects of yourself which have been hidden from you. It will help you face your fears, connect with undiscovered gifts, and awaken to your soul's message. As you discover more of who you really are, you will gain a new understanding of the mythology of your own life."

Dixie Gladstone,
FeminineAstrology.com

Women's Studies
Psychology Self-Help

ISBN 9780982500088

90000 >

9 780982 500088

Parallel Curriculum Units

for

Mathematics

Grades 6–12

Jann H. Leppien | Jeanne H. Purcell

EDITORS